The Children of
EGYPT

MIDDLE EAST STUDIES CENTER
PORTLAND STATE UNIVERSITY
P.O. BOX 751
PORTLAND, OR 97207-0751

THE WORLD'S CHILDREN

The Children of
EGYPT

MATTI A. PITKÄNEN
WITH REIJO HÄRKÖNEN

Carolrhoda Books, Inc./Minneapolis

*The publisher wishes to thank Nassif Youssif, Head of the Middle East
Library at the University of Minnesota, for his assistance with the
preparation of this book.*

This edition first published 1991 by Carolrhoda Books, Inc.
First published in Finland in 1986 by Otava Publishing Company Ltd.
under the title FAARAOIDEN PERILLISET.
Original edition copyright © 1986 by Matti A. Pitkänen
Additional text copyright © 1991 by Carolrhoda Books, Inc.

Library of Congress Cataloging-in-Publication Data

Härkönen, Reijo.

  [Faaraoiden perilliset. English]
  The children of Egypt / by Reijo Härkönen ; photographs by Matti
A. Pitkänen.
     p.   cm. – (The World's children)
  Translation of: Faaraoiden perilliset.
  Summary: Provides an introduction to Egypt and its people, with a
special focus on the day-to-day life of the children.
  ISBN 0-87614-396-6
  1. Egypt–Juvenile literature. 2. Children–Egypt–Juvenile
literature. [1. Egypt. 2. Egypt–Social life and customs.]
I. Pitkänen, Matti A., ill. II. Title. III. Series: The World's
children (Minneapolis, Minn.)
DT49.H2513   1991
962–dc20   90-42221
                                                      CIP
                                                       AC

Manufactured in the United States of America

   2   3   4   5   6   7   8   9   10   00   99   98   97   96   95   94   93

The waters of the Nile River sparkle in the early morning sunlight. It promises to be another scorching day, like the day before, and the day before that. The only sound is the tapping of a hammer against a chisel as a young man carves pictures in a wall of stone. The place is the Egyptian city of Thebes. The time is the 15th century B.C.—nearly 3,500 years ago.

Egypt was one of the first places in the world to be settled. On that sunny morning in Thebes so long ago, the Egyptians had already lived in the Nile Valley for more than 1,500 years. By that time, Egypt was the most powerful civilization in the world, and Thebes was its capital city.

Thebes is no longer Egypt's capital. The modern capital of Egypt is Cairo, another city on the Nile River. All that is left of Thebes are the temples and monuments that are still standing thousands of years after their creators have died.

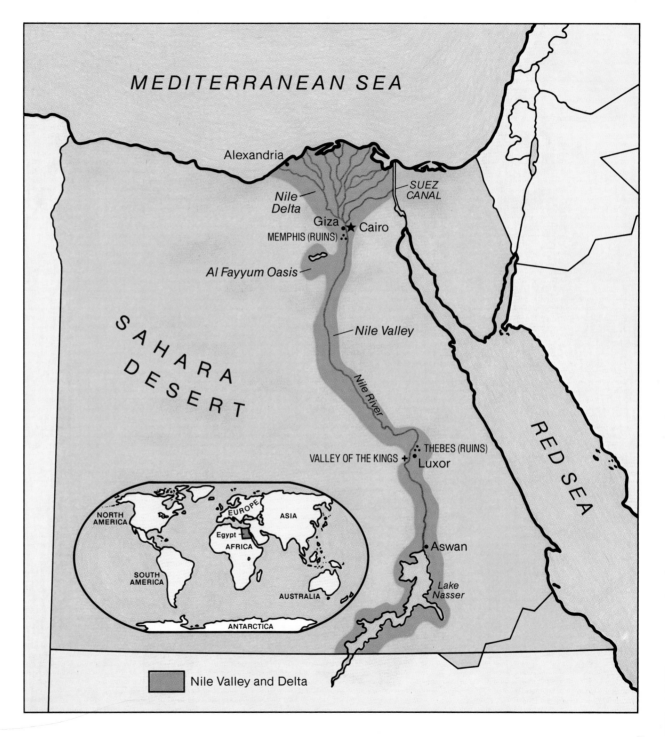

The young man carving pictures in the wall might have been working on a project for Thutmose III, the pharaoh—or ruler—of Egypt at that time.

Egypt's ancient monuments are covered with the stories of its pharaohs. But the tales are not written with letters like *A, B,* and *C.* The ancient Egyptians used a kind of writing called hieroglyphics, which used pictures instead of letters. The name Thutmose III was written with a picture of the sun, a god, and a beetle.

The pharaohs are probably more famous for the way they died than the way they lived. Ancient Egyptians were very concerned about what happened to people after they died. The pharaohs built huge tombs for themselves and filled them with clothes and jewels and even food to use in the afterlife. Many of these tombs were built near Thebes in an area called the Valley of the Kings.

There is an ancient Egyptian tale about a fisherman who was afraid that he would be eaten by one of the crocodiles that lived in the Nile. The fisherman's story was written on papyrus, the world's first "paper." Now, 4,000 years later, the papyrus is brown and brittle, but the story survives. This durable writing material was also used as a canvas for colorful paintings of pharaohs and gods.

Papyrus was made from the stem of the shaggy-looking papyrus plant, which grows on the banks of the Nile River. The stems were flattened out and pressed together into sheets. The ancient Egyptians wrote with reed brushes dipped in ink made of water and soot.

Like the stories carved on the temple walls, the fisherman's tale was written in hieroglyphics. The ancient Egyptians used hieroglyphic writing for about 3,000 years, before they replaced it with a simpler writing system after the fourth century A.D.

Said is learning how to sail a felucca, an Egyptian sailboat. He would like to be a boatman like his father when he grows up. The wind in the felucca's sail carries them up the Nile River. They will not need to use the sail for the return trip because the Nile's current will carry them home.

Feluccas are used to carry passengers and merchandise. Said and his father started their day early in the morning. Now the sun is high in the sky, their boat is full, and the river bustles with activity.

Feluccas have sailed the waters of the Nile for thousands of years. In modern times, the felucca shares the river with motorboats and cruise ships. These modern boats are much faster and more comfortable than the ancient sailboat, but they are not nearly as graceful.

The Nile is the longest river in the world. It winds its way through northeastern Africa like a long, blue snake, finally bringing its life-giving waters to Egypt. The river's journey covers more than 4,000 miles.

Nearly all Egyptians live in the Nile Valley—a narrow strip of land on either side of the river—or in the Nile Delta—the place where the river fans out into several smaller channels before entering the Mediterranean Sea.

The Nile is the center of life in Egypt because it is one of the few sources of water. Except for the land near the Nile River, most of Egypt is desert. People wash their clothes—and themselves—in the river. Many also depend on the Nile for drinking water.

Because it almost never rains in Egypt, farmers must use water from the Nile to irrigate their crops. One ancient irrigation device that is still used is the sakia, which is a kind of waterwheel. An animal harnessed to the sakia walks around in a circle, turning the wheel. The sakia's buckets scoop up river water and pour it onto the fields. Watering the crops is a never-ending job under Egypt's hot sun.

Hamed lives near Cairo in one of the many villages that line the banks of the Nile. Hamed's village is very old. Its mud-brick houses are crowded onto narrow, winding streets that are almost always filled with people and animals.

In newer villages, the houses are built from blocks of stone instead of brick, and the streets are wide and straight. But these streets are also filled with people. So many people live on the little bits of land along the Nile that they have grown used to living close together.

Like most Egyptians, Hamed has a large family. They have outgrown their house, so they are building a new one. The new house will have three rooms and a central courtyard. Building a house is a big job, so the whole family helps. They form bricks out of mud and leave them to dry in the sun. When the bricks are dry and hard, the building can begin.

Mud is also used to make another kind of house—a pigeon house. These large, knobby structures—called dovecotes—can be found throughout the Egyptian countryside. In Egypt, pigeons are raised for their meat, which is stuffed with rice and spices and roasted.

Most Egyptians can't afford to eat meat very often. Other foods that come from animals, including milk and eggs, are also very expensive.

The two foods that nearly every Egyptian eats are bread and beans. The Egyptian national dish is a paste made of ground-up beans and other ingredients such as oil and spices. It is usually eaten with bread.

In the countryside, breadmaking can be a social occasion. Women gather to catch up on the news of the village while mixing, shaping, and baking bread. Traditional Egyptian bread is round and flat. Some breads are hard and dry, others are soft and might have a pocket that can be filled with food.

Aziza lives near Luxor, only a few miles from the ruins of the city of Thebes. Her family grows beans and corn to eat and to sell. They also grow clover to feed to their animals. Aziza's family has a goat to give them milk and a water buffalo to pull the plow. Her mother also raises chickens for eggs.

Aziza's family has only two acres to farm. It is hard to raise enough food to feed the entire family on such a small space, but they are lucky to have any land at all. The Nile Valley and Delta have become so crowded that most people must farm land that belongs to someone else or find something else to do besides farming. More and more people are leaving the countryside to look for jobs in the city. Aziza doesn't want to move to the city. She likes living in the country, where life is peaceful.

It is late afternoon and the sun is a golden glow in the western sky. In the streets of Luxor, a barber gives one of his regular customers a close shave, and a fruit seller sips a cup of tea while his customers examine his wares.

Most of the people in the street are dressed in galabiyas, which are long, flowing robes. While many Egyptians still wear these traditional garments, Western-style clothes, such as suits and dresses, are becoming more and more popular, especially in the city.

Nearly every day as evening approaches, Aziza's father meets some of his friends at a coffeehouse in Luxor. They talk over the day's events while enjoying good strong coffee with plenty of sugar.

23

Once a week, Aziza gets up very early in the morning to go to the bazaar, which is an outdoor market. Aziza's whole family goes to the bazaar, even the baby.

The bazaar is already quite crowded and noisy when they arrive. People spread out their wares and call out greetings to friends. Aziza helps her mother display the vegetables and eggs she will sell that day. Meanwhile, Aziza's sister Sahar looks after the baby.

Aziza likes to listen to her mother as she bargains with each customer to get the best price for her wares. Only food is sold at this bazaar. There are other markets in nearby Luxor where people can buy rugs, spices, pottery, and even toys.

On Tuesdays, there is a different kind of market in Luxor. At this market, people display camels, goats, cows, and donkeys instead of potatoes and oranges. The animals that are sold will be used for their meat or their milk, or perhaps to plow a field or pull a wagon.

The people who are selling the animals are all men. In most of Egypt, it is traditional for men to make the money to support their families. While women may sell a few things at the market, their main responsibility is to take care of the home and the children. These traditions are slowly changing, though, especially in the city, where both men and women are likely to have jobs.

Samira, Aida, and Efra have come to the market to watch. They like the baby animals the best. Aida is holding the smallest animal at the market, a tiny goat kid that is only a few weeks old.

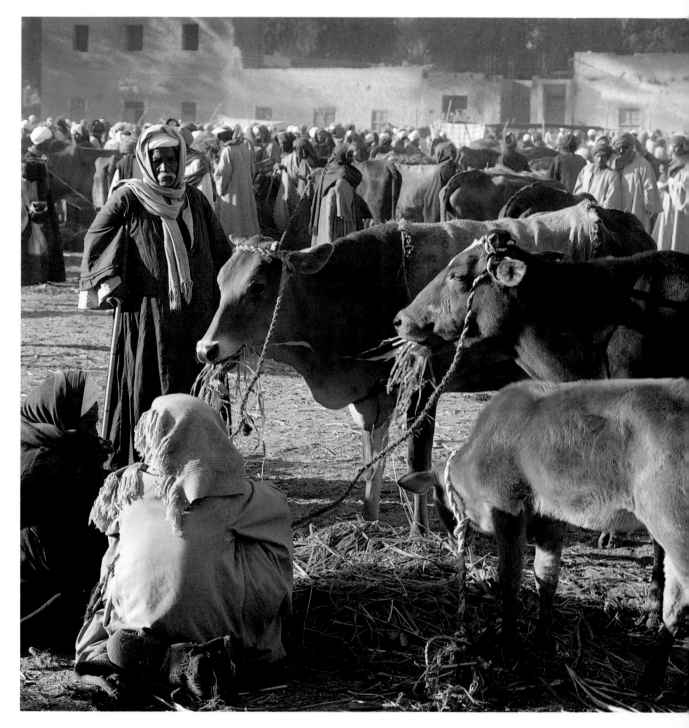

A few miles either west or east of the Nile, the fields suddenly give way to huge, craggy rocks and sand that seems to go on forever. This is the great Sahara Desert, the largest desert in the world.

Although the desert may look uninhabited, it is home to a small number of people called Bedouins. Bedouins are herders who raise sheep, goats, and camels. Many of these people don't live in one spot, but travel from place to place, always looking for fresh pasture for their animals.

Although many of the desert people now use cars or trucks for transportation, the traditional mount of the Bedouin is the camel. Camels are ideally suited for the desert. Their large, padded feet are secure on constantly shifting sand, and they are able to go days without water. But their rolling walk makes for a very bumpy ride, and their grunts and groans let their riders know that they don't especially enjoy their work.

29

Muhammad lives on the Fayyum Oasis. An oasis is a patch of vegetation that exists as if by magic in the middle of the desert. The "magic" is actually some source of water that makes it possible for plants to grow.

Life on an oasis is no different from life in other parts of Egypt. In the morning, Muhammad goes to school. He loves to learn about the rich history of his country. Muhammad's teacher told him that thousands of years ago, there was a city on the Fayyum Oasis called Crocodilopolis. People would come from as far away as Europe to feed the sacred crocodiles that lived on the oasis.

Some of Muhammad's friends don't go to school at all. They work in the fields all day instead. But Muhammad's parents, who never learned how to read or write, want each one of their sons and daughters to get a good education. They say that there is plenty of time for them to help in the fields in the afternoon when school is done for the day.

Egypt's capital is about an hour's drive from the Fayyum Oasis. Every time Muhammad visits Cairo, he is surprised by the noise and activity of this crowded city. The streets are usually jammed with cars, with horns honking and radios blasting. And there are people everywhere—on the sidewalks, in the streets, in the windows, and even on some of the rooftops.

Cairo is both a modern and an ancient city. In the western half, there are modern apartments, shops, and office buildings. Many of the people from this part of the city have adopted Western ways.

Eastern Cairo is the older, more traditional section of the city. Its narrow streets are lined with open-front shops. Over the shops are tiny apartments. Many of the people who live in eastern Cairo have moved to the city from the country to try to make a better living. Some work in factories, others sell goods at bazaars, but few have very much money at all.

The slender spires, called minarets, and the shining silver domes of the Muhammad Ali Mosque soar into the sky near the center of Cairo. The building is also known as the Alabaster Mosque because it is made out of beautiful cream-colored stone.

A mosque is a Muslim house of worship. There are hundreds of mosques in the city of Cairo alone. Most Egyptians are Muslim.

Five times a day, beginning at dawn and ending at nightfall, men called muezzins climb to the top of the minarets of Cairo's mosques and call Muslims to prayer. Some people go to a mosque to pray, and others stop what they are doing and kneel down wherever they are. When they are done praying, people go on their way until the next call to prayer.

Just across the Nile from Cairo is the most famous reminder of Egypt's past. Perched on a hill near the town of Giza are three gigantic pyramids guarded by the Great Sphinx, an enormous statue of a creature that appears to be half man and half lion.

The pyramids are tombs that were built for three pharaohs almost 4,500 years ago. The largest pyramid is called the Great Pyramid. It is made up of more than two million limestone blocks, each weighing about as much as a small car.

Although there are other famous pyramids in Egypt, people come from all over the world to visit the pyramids at Giza. Ahmad earns extra money for his family by giving people horseback rides from one pyramid to another. Others offer camel rides to the more adventurous.

Even after a long day, Ahmad never tires of watching the people who are seeing the pyramids for the first time. As the setting sun slips behind the pyramids, just as it has for thousands of years, Ahmad is proud to live in the land of the pharaohs—he is proud to be an Egyptian.

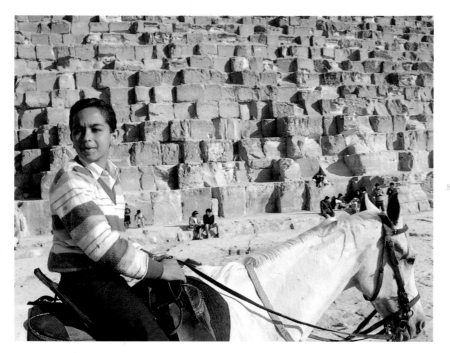

More about Egypt

What is Egypt's official name?
Egypt's official name is the Arab Republic of Egypt.

What is the capital of Egypt?
Cairo has been Egypt's capital city for about a thousand years. Other cities that have served as Egypt's capital include Memphis, Thebes, and Alexandria. Memphis and Thebes no longer exist.

How many people live in Egypt?
Egypt is home to about 54,000,000 people.

How big is Egypt?
The area of Egypt is 386,662 square miles. This is about the size of the states of Texas and New Mexico combined.

What is Egypt's official language?
Egypt's official language is Arabic.

What religion is followed by most Egyptians?
About 90 percent of all Egyptians are Muslim. Egypt's next largest religious group is the Coptic Christians, who make up more than 5 percent of the population.

Pronunciation Guide

bazaar buh-ZAHR
Bedouin BEHD-uh-wihn
Cairo KY-roh
Crocodilopolis crahk-oh-dihl-AH-poh-lihs
Fayyum Oasis fy-YOOM oh-AY-sihs
felucca fee-LOO-kah
galabiya juh-lah-BEE-yah
Giza GEE-zuh
hieroglyphics hy-ruh-GLIHF-ihks
Luxor LUHK-suhr
mosque mahsk
muezzin myoo-EHZ'n
Muhammad Ali moo-HAHM-ahd AH-lee
papyrus puh-PY-ruhs
pharaoh FEH-roh
sakia SACK-yah
Sphinx SFINGKS
Thebes THEEBZ
Thutmose thoot-MOH-suh

Index

MIDDLE EAST STUDIES CENTER
PORTLAND STATE UNIVERSITY
P.O. BOX 751
PORTLAND, OR 97207-0751